GINGER

GINGER
A BOOK OF RECIPES

HELEN SUDELL

LORENZ BOOKS

This edition is published by Lorenz Books,
an imprint of Anness Publishing Ltd,
108 Great Russell Street, London WC1B 3NA;
info@anness.com

www.lorenzbooks.com; www.annesspublishing.com

If you like the images in this book and would like to investigate
using them for publishing, promotions or advertising, please visit
our website www.practicalpictures.com for more information

© Anness Publishing Limited 2014

A CIP catalogue record for this book is available from
The British Library

Publisher Joanna Lorenz
Editorial Director Helen Sudell
Designer Nigel Partridge
Illustrations Anna Koska

Photographers: Martin Brigdale, Steve Moss, William Lingwood,
Craig Robertson, Charlie Richards, Gus Filgate, Simon Smith,
Debbie Patterson, Frank Adam, John Whitaker, Nicki Dowey
Recipes by: Sunil Vijayakar, Ghillie Basan, Joanna Farrow,
Vilma Laus, Stuart Walton, Georgina Campbell, Terry Tan,
Mridula Baljekar, Janet Laurence, Young Jin Song, Judy Bastyra,
Becky Johnson, Jenny White, Claire Ptak, Carol Pastor,
Mirko Trenkner, Nicola Graimes, Mowie Kay

COOK'S NOTES
• Bracketed terms are intended for American readers.

• For all recipes, quantities are given in both metric and imperial
measures and, where appropriate, in standard cups and spoons.
Follow one set of measures, but not a mixture, because they are
not interchangeable.

• Standard spoon and cup measures are level. 1 tsp = 5ml,
1 tbsp = 15ml, 1 cup = 250ml/8fl oz.

• Australian standard tablespoons are 20ml. Australian readers
should use 3 tsp in place of 1 tbsp for measuring small quantities.

• American pints are 16fl oz/2 cups. American readers should use
20fl oz/2.5 cups in place of 1 pint when measuring liquids.

• Electric oven temperatures in this book are for conventional
ovens. When using a fan oven, the temperature will probably
need to be reduced by about 10–20°C/20–40°F. Since ovens
vary, you should check with your manufacturer's instruction
book for guidance.

• The nutritional analysis given for each recipe is calculated per
portion (i.e. serving or item), unless otherwise stated. If the recipe
gives a range, such as Serves 4–6, then the nutritional analysis will
be for the smaller portion size, i.e. 6 servings. The analysis does not
include optional ingredients, such as salt added to taste.

• Medium (US large) eggs are used unless otherwise stated.

PUBLISHER'S NOTE

CONTENTS

INTRODUCTION

Who has not stopped to savour the delicious smell of ginger cooking? Whether it is the comforting and homely aroma of gingerbread baking on a winter's day or an intriguing burst of oriental promise, ginger has immediate appeal for both sweet and savoury meals, all year round. When you cut into a piece of fresh root ginger you are instantly hit with a hint of lemon with a refreshing sharpness. Jamaican ginger is said to have the finest aroma,

Below: Grating ginger results in a soft paste.

with the Kenyan spice being of good quality too. Other African and Indian gingers have a darker skin and a biting, perhaps less pleasant flavour.

Another member of the ginger family, galangal, grows in India and south-east Asia where it is an essential ingredient in many dishes. In the West, it has only become widely available as a fresh spice over the past twenty years or so.

COOKING WITH GINGER

Ginger has been a kitchen staple for more than a millennium – its use in Chinese cooking dates back to 2000BC. It is sold as a fresh root, dried whole, ground to powder, preserved in syrup and crystallized. Each form has a subtly different flavour, but common to all is a sweet and pungent spiciness.

Powdered ginger journeyed to northern Europe early: its associations were, historically,

Above: Ginger adds a hint of spice to sweet preserves.

wintery, bringing cheer at the coldest time of year. Gingerbread is one of the oldest cake-breads in the world and is now usually associated with Christmas and other winter festivals. Stem ginger, preserved in syrup in handsome blue and white jars that are now prized in their own right, came to Europe early in the eighteenth century from China.

Ginger is used in most of Asia, and its flavour is central to the characteristic spice blends of a wide variety of oriental cuisines. Ginger, garlic and spring onions (scallions) are the classic note of Chinese recipes; in India, the combination of ginger with onions and garlic is evident in north Indian sauces and in the vegetarian dishes that are the delight of southern states such as Gujarat. Powdered ginger is included in spice mixes and is popular in the rich dishes of Mogul cuisine – as it is also in Moroccan cooking. With the rise in popularity of Japanese and south-east Asian cooking the use of ginger has also increased.

Galangal, both the lesser and greater varieties, is mostly used in seafood and chicken dishes. It is frequently pounded with onion, garlic and chillies to make a spice paste. Slices are added to Thai soups and curries.

THERAPEUTIC USES

Henry VIII is said to have used ginger for its medicinal qualities, as outlined by the herbalist, Culpeper, 150 years

later: "Ginger helps digestion, warms the stomach, clears the sight, and is profitable for old men; it heats the joints and is therefore useful against gout." Ginger has an impressive record in treating all kinds of ailments: it is said to help circulation, and also to cure flatulence and indigestion; it is taken as a drink for coughs, nausea and influenza. Many pregnant women swear by it to help ease the effect of morning sickness. In the East, ginger is chewed to ward off evil spirits and to help alleviate travel sickness.

GINGERBREAD TRADITION

The technique of making gingerbread houses began during the Middle Ages when gingerbread became popular in Europe. The Bavarian city of Nuremberg became known as the gingerbread capital of the world . Here, the art of carving ornate gingerbread shapes was developed. The gingerbread was carved into shapes of kings and queens, windmills, letters, stars

and hearts. When baked, they were frequently gilded with gold paint, studded with spices and dried fruits and sold at markets and fairs.

The German fairy tale 'Hansel and Gretel', in which the children, whilst walking in a forest, discover a house made entirely of gingerbread, candies and cake, inspired the trend for making beautiful constructions based on gingerbread. These have a fairy-tale appearance, dusted with sugar and traditionally presented to friends at Christmas.

Below: Decorated gingerbread is a popular gift at Christmas.

TYPES OF GINGER

FRESH ROOT GINGER
A fresh knobbly root with a smooth, plump appearance and a pale tan-coloured skin. Any wrinkling indicates that the ginger is past its best. The most delicate flesh of the ginger is just below the skin.

DRIED ROOT GINGER
This is very different from the fresh form, and is no substitute for fresh root ginger. The whole root can be used in mixtures of pickling spices and requires bruising to release the flavour.

CRYSTALLIZED GINGER
Ginger is preserved in sugar syrup and then thickly coated in crystallized sugar and used as a flavouring in baking, or added to desserts such as ice cream.

GROUND GINGER
The ground form of dried ginger root has a hot, spicy flavour and is an essential spice in cakes, gingerbread and ginger biscuits. It is also used in savoury dishes such as curries and soups.

STEM GINGER
Tender, young shoots of ginger are cooked and preserved in sugar syrup. Both the ginger and the syrup can be used in cakes, sauces and ice creams. The syrup can be added to marinades for savoury dishes to give a sweet, gingery flavour.

PICKLED GINGER
Chinese pickled ginger is preserved in sweetened vinegar and is light, sweet-sour and quite hot in flavour. It is often

eaten as an appetizer or used in cooking. Japanese pickled ginger is more delicate, and there are two types: one is red, one pale pink, but both have traditional savoury roles.

GINGER PULP
To make ginger pulp peel about 225g/8oz fresh root ginger and place in a food processor or blender. Process until pulped, adding a little water if necessary. Store in an airtight container in the refrigerator for up to 6 weeks and use as needed.

GALANGAL
The galangals (greater and lesser) are grown in India and south-east Asia. Greater galangal has a pine-like aroma and a pungent flavour. Lesser galangal is distinctly more aromatic with a strong peppery taste, so only a little is needed.

Left: Galangal is used to flavour curries and savoury soups.

Crystallized ginger

Fresh root ginger

Stem ginger

Sliced ginger

Fresh root ginger

Pickled ginger

Dried root ginger

Ground ginger

Ginger pulp

BASIC TECHNIQUES AND RECIPES

All you really need to prepare ginger is a good, small, sharp knife and a chopping board.

PREPARING GINGER

1 Thinly peel or scrape off the skin from a piece of fresh root ginger.

2 Grate the root, taking care not to graze your fingers in the process. Peeled ginger can be ground to a paste with garlic, other spices and a little oil.

3 Cut thin, peeled slices into matchstick strips for use in stir-fries or similar dishes. The strips can be cut across to provide coarsely chopped ginger or can be chopped in a food processor.

4 If the fresh root ginger is to be used in a stir-fry, heat the wok, then add the oil. When the oil is hot, add the chopped or grated ginger and any other ingredients and stir-fry for 30 seconds until the ginger is just golden brown.

PICKLED GINGER
This pickle is often served with broths, noodles and rice.

Peel 225g/8oz fresh young ginger, sprinkle with 10ml/2 tsp salt, cover and place in the refrigerator for 24 hours. Drain off any liquid and pat dry. Slice the ginger very finely along the grain and place them in a sterilized jar. In a small bowl beat 200ml/7fl oz/1 cup white rice vinegar with 50g/2oz/¼ cup sugar, until it has dissolved. Pour the pickling liquid over the ginger and cover. Store in the refrigerator or in a cool place for about a week.

GINGER AND HOISIN DIP

Chunky and bursting with flavour, this dip is delicious with prawn (shrimp) crackers.

Serves 4

Mix 60ml/4 tbsp hoisin sauce with 120ml/4fl oz/½ cup passata (bottled strained tomatoes) in a bowl. Thinly slice 4 spring onions (scallions); peel and finely chop 5cm/1½in piece of fresh root ginger; seed and chop 2 fresh red chillies and crush 2 garlic cloves. Stir in the spring onions, ginger, chillies and garlic into the hoisin sauce mix. Add 5ml/ 1 tsp sesame oil, mix well and serve. It can be stored in the refrigerator for up to 1 week.

LEMON GRASS AND GINGER JELLY

This aromatic jelly is delicious with Asian-style roast meat and poultry such as Chinese crispy duck. It is also the perfect foil for rich fish, especially cold smoked trout or mackerel.

Makes about 900g/2lb

Using a rolling pin, bruise 2 lemon grass stalks and chop them roughly. Put the chopped lemon grass in a preserving pan and pour over 1.5kg/2½ pints/ 6¼ cups water.

Add 1.3kg/3lb lemons (washed and cut into small pieces) and 50g/2oz fresh root ginger (unpeeled and thinly sliced). Bring to the boil, then reduce the heat, cover and simmer for 1 hour, until the lemons are pulpy.

Pour the fruit and juices into a sterilized jelly bag suspended over a large bowl. Leave to drain for at least 3 hours, or until the juice stops dripping.

Measure the juice into the cleaned preserving pan, adding 450g/1lb/2¼ cups sugar for every 600ml/1 pint/2½ cups juice. Heat the mixture gently, stirring occasionally, until the sugar has dissolved completely. Boil rapidly for about 10 minutes until the jelly reaches setting point (105°C/220°F). Remove the jelly mixture from the heat.

Skim any scum off the surface using a slotted spoon, then pour the jelly into warmed sterilized jars, cover and seal. Store in a cool, dark place and use within 1 year. Once opened, keep in the refrigerator and consume within 3 months.

GINGER DRINKS

Ginger adds a gentle spiciness to both hot and cold drinks. It helps to aid digestion and soothe upset stomachs.

GINGER BEER

Making ginger beer at home is relatively easy, although you do need to allow 3 days for the mixture to rest.

Bruise 40g/1½ oz root ginger to release the flavour. Finely peel 1 lemon, squeeze out the juice and reserve. Place the ginger, lemon rind (zest) and 25g/1 oz cream of tartar into a large bowl. Pour over 4.5 litres/ 8 pints boiling water, and the reserved lemon juice. Allow to cool to room temperature, mix in 25g/1oz brewers yeast and stir well to mix.

Cover the container with a clean cloth and secure with string or elastic. Leave in a warm place for 24 hours. Skim off the froth and use a jug or pitcher to bale out the liquid, taking care not to disturb the sediment. Pour the ginger beer into sterilized bottles and stopper tightly. Store the bottles in a cool, dark place for 3 days, when the ginger beer will be ready to drink.

STEM GINGER AND PEAR SHAKE

Preserved stem ginger makes the perfect partner to juicy pears in this light and creamy summer creation.

Slice 3 pieces preserved stem ginger, reserving a few thin slices and 30ml/1 tbsp ginger syrup from the jar. Drain 400g/14oz can pears in natural fruit juice, reserving 150l/¼ pint/⅔ cup of the juice. Put the pears, measured juice and chopped ginger in a blender or food processor and blend until smooth.

Strain through a sieve into a jug or pitcher. Whisk in 150ml/¼ pint/⅔ cup full cream (whole) milk, 100ml/3½ fl oz/scant ½ cup single (light) cream and ginger syrup and pour into long two chilled glasses. Serve immediately, scattered with the reserved thin ginger slices.

Shortly before serving, add some ice cubes and 1.2 litres/2 pints/5 cups ginger beer to the jug and decorate with lemon slices or sprigs of fresh mint. Serve in tall glasses.

GINGER TEA

A cup of hot ginger tea is warming and soothing and is easy to make using pieces of crystallized ginger.

Add 2.5ml/½ tsp clear honey, 2.5ml/½ tsp ground cinnamon and a slice of lemon to 1 teacup of hot black tea. Drop in 2 pieces of crystallized (candied) ginger and leave for two minutes. Drink while still warm.

KIWI AND GINGER SPRITZER

Ginger and kiwi fruits combine beautifully in this refreshing summer drink.

Slice 1 piece of preserved stem ginger finely and peel and then roughly chop 2 kiwi fruits, reserving a few thin slices. Push the ginger and then the kiwi fruit through a juicer and pour it into a jug or pitcher. Stir in 15ml/1 tbsp syrup from the preserved stem ginger jar. Pour the juice into a tall glass, then top up with sparkling mineral water and serve immediately with the reserved kiwi slices.

APPLE AND GINGER PRESSÉ

This refreshing cocktail uses pressed apple juice and ginger beer for a winning combination.

Mix 1.2 litres/2 pints/5 cups unsweetened apple juice with the juice of 1 lemon in a large jug or pitcher. Wash and core 4 small red-skinned eating apples but do not peel them. Slice thinly and add the slices to the jug.

Stir well and, to prevent browning, check that all the slices are immersed. Cover and set aside in the refrigerator to chill until required.

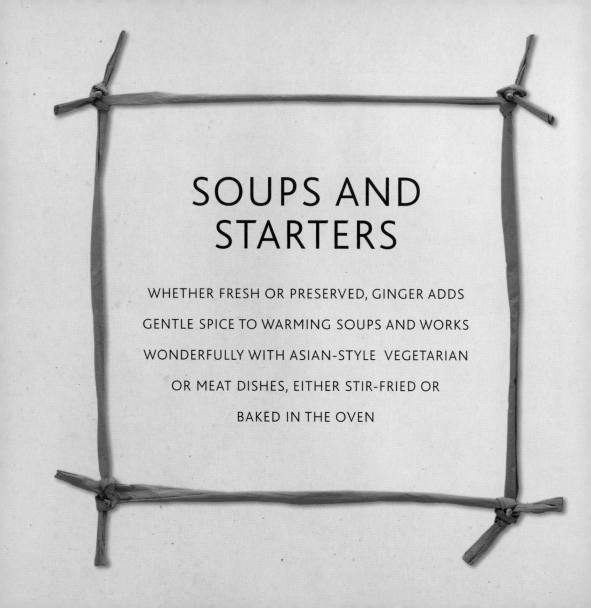

SOUPS AND STARTERS

WHETHER FRESH OR PRESERVED, GINGER ADDS

GENTLE SPICE TO WARMING SOUPS AND WORKS

WONDERFULLY WITH ASIAN-STYLE VEGETARIAN

OR MEAT DISHES, EITHER STIR-FRIED OR

BAKED IN THE OVEN

EGG DROP AND GINGER SOUP

This soup is very easy to make, nutritious and beautifully light; the sort of thing that would be served at home to refresh the palate between more elaborate dishes.

Serves 4
750ml/1¼ pints/3 cups fresh vegetable stock
30ml/2 tbsp finely shredded fresh root ginger
2 eggs
30ml/2 tbsp Chinese rice wine
chopped spring onions (scallions) or fresh coriander (cilantro), to garnish

> **VARIATION**
> For more substance, soak a handful of cellophane noodles in boiling water for 5 minutes. Drain and add to the soup just before dropping in the egg. This version is filling enough to serve as a light meal.

Energy 44kcal/184kJ; Protein 3.3g; Carbohydrate 0.2g, of which sugars 0.1g; Fat 2.9g, of which saturates 0.8g; Cholesterol 95mg; Calcium 18mg; Fibre 0.1g; Sodium 166mg.

Bring the stock to the boil in a medium pan. Add the finely shredded ginger and cook for 3 minutes.

Meanwhile, beat the eggs in a bowl. Pour them into the boiling soup in a steady stream, using a fork or chopsticks to stir the surface at the same time. As it cooks, the egg will set, forming long shreds or strands.

Stir in the rice wine. Ladle into bowls, garnish with the spring onions or coriander, and serve hot.

VEGETABLES IN CHILLI, GINGER AND GARLIC BROTH

This delicate vegetable soup is created without using any fat. Instead it relies upon the use of fresh herbs and spices to produce a superb, distinctive flavour.

Serves 4

250g/9oz/1 cup potatoes, cut into 2.5cm/1in cubes
1–2 green chillies, sliced diagonally (seeded if you like)
150g/5oz/1 cup green beans, cut into 2.5cm/1in lengths
150g/5oz/1 cup green cabbage, coarsely chopped
1 tsp salt or to taste
2 tsp grated fresh root ginger
1 large garlic clove, crushed
150g/5oz/1 cup fresh spinach, roughly chopped
1–2 tbsp coriander (cilantro) leaves, chopped

Energy 77kcal/322kJ; Protein 3.7g; Carbohydrate 14.1g, of which sugars 4.4g; Fat 0.9g, of which saturates 0.2g; Cholesterol 0mg; Calcium 125mg; Fibre 3.7g; Sodium 66mg.

Put the potatoes in a medium-sized pan, pour in 700ml/1¼ pints/ 3 cups water and bring to the boil. Add the chillies, reduce the heat to low, cover and cook for 7–8 minutes.

Add the green beans and cabbage, bring back to the boil, cover and cook over a medium heat for 5 minutes. Add the salt, ginger and garlic, put the lid back on the pan and continue to cook for another 5 minutes.

Stir in the spinach and cook for a further 1–2 minutes until it has wilted. Add the coriander leaves, cook for about 1 minute, then remove from the heat and serve.

ARTICHOKE HEARTS WITH GINGER AND LEMON

This dish comes from Morocco where globe artichokes are a favourite first course. Here they are cooked in a glorious spiced ginger and lemon dressing.

Serves 4
30–45ml/2–3 tbsp olive oil
2 garlic cloves, crushed
scant 5ml/1 tsp ground ginger
pinch of saffron threads
juice of ½ lemon
peel of 1 preserved lemon, finely sliced
8 artichoke hearts, quartered
150ml/¼ pint/½ cup water
salt

Heat the olive oil in a small heavy pan and stir in the garlic. Before the garlic begins to colour, stir in the ginger, saffron, lemon juice, and preserved lemon peel. Add the artichokes and toss them in the spices. Pour in the water, add a little salt and heat until simmering.

Cover the pan and simmer for 10–15 minutes until the artichokes are tender, turning them occasionally. If the liquid has not reduced, take the lid off the pan and boil for about 2 minutes until reduced to a coating consistency. Serve warm or at room temperature.

Energy 142kcal/586kJ; Protein 1.6g; Carbohydrate 4.1g, of which sugars 1.9g; Fat 11.3g, of which saturates 1.6g; Cholesterol 0mg; Calcium 40mg; Fibre 1.6g; Sodium 47mg.

PREPARING GLOBE ARTICHOKES
Remove the outer leaves and cut off the stems. Carefully separate the remaining leaves and use a teaspoon to scoop out the choke with all the hairy bits. Trim the hearts and immerse them in water mixed with a squeeze of lemon juice to prevent them from turning black.

GOLDEN MUNG BEAN PATTIES

Skinless split mung beans are ground and cooked with spices until reaching a mashed potato-like consistency. The mixture is then formed into small round cakes and deep-fried until crisp and golden.

Makes 12

250g/9oz/1½ cups skinless split mung beans (mung dhal)
2.5cm/1in piece of fresh root ginger, roughly chopped
1–2 dried red chillies, chopped
1 tsp ground turmeric
1 tbsp coriander (cilantro) leaves, chopped
1 green chilli, finely chopped (seeded if you like)
50g/2oz natural (plain) yogurt
¾ tsp salt or to taste
oil for deep frying
chutney, to serve

Wash the mung beans in 2–3 changes of water and soak for 3–4 hours. Drain and put them in a food processor with the ginger and red chillies. Grind to a slightly coarse consistency, then transfer to a non-stick pan over a low heat. Add the turmeric and cook, stirring, until the mixture is dry and slightly crumbly.

Remove from the heat and add all the remaining ingredients except the oil. Mix thoroughly and make 12 equal balls, then flatten them into neat, round cakes.

Heat the oil in a wok or other suitable pan for frying over a low/medium heat. Fry the patties until they are golden brown. Serve with any chutney.

Energy 148kcal/620kJ; Protein 5.4g; Carbohydrate 12.6g, of which sugars 0.8g; Fat 8.9g, of which saturates 1g; Cholesterol 0mg; Calcium 22mg; Fibre 1g; Sodium 12mg.

CARAMELIZED CHICKEN WINGS WITH GINGER

Cooked in a wok or in the oven, these caramelized wings are flavoured with ginger and drizzled with chilli oil then eaten with the fingers, with every bit of tender meat sucked off the bone.

Serves 4

75ml/5 tbsp sugar
30ml/2 tbsp groundnut (peanut) oil
25g/1oz fresh root ginger, peeled and finely shredded or grated
12 chicken wings, split in two
chilli oil, for drizzling
mixed pickled vegetables, to serve

To make a caramel sauce, gently heat the sugar with 60ml/4 tbsp water in a small, heavy pan until it turns golden. Set aside.

Heat the oil in a wok or heavy pan. Add the ginger and stir-fry until fragrant. Add the chicken wings and toss them around the wok to cover them in the oil, and brown.

Pour in the caramel sauce and make sure the chicken wings are coated in it. Reduce the heat, cover the wok or pan, and cook for about 30 minutes, until tender, and the sauce has caramelized.

Drizzle chilli oil over the wings and serve from the wok or pan with mixed pickled vegetables.

Energy 393Kcal/1641kJ; Protein 30.5g;
Carbohydrate 14.4g, of which sugars 14.4g;
Fat 24g, of which saturates 6.3g;
Cholesterol 134mg; Calcium 16mg; Fibre
0g; Sodium 100mg

SPARE RIBS WITH GINGER

Spicy and sweet sticky ribs are a popular choice to start an informal weekday meal with family or friends. Choose the meatiest ribs you can, to make them a real success.

Serves 8

1kg/2¼ lb pork spare ribs
10ml/2 tsp Chinese five-spice powder
2 garlic cloves, crushed
15ml/1 tbsp grated fresh root ginger, plus extra fine strips to garnish
2.5ml/½ tsp chilli sauce
60ml/4 tbsp muscovado (molasses) sugar
15ml/1 tbsp sunflower oil
5 spring onions (scallions), to serve
green salad leaves, to serve

If the spare ribs are still joined together, neatly cut between them to separate them (or ask your butcher to do this). Place the spare ribs in a large bowl.

Mix together all the remaining ingredients, except the spring onions and salad leaves, and pour over the ribs. Toss well to coat evenly. Cover the bowl and leave to marinate in the refrigerator overnight.

Heat a wok or large frying pan, place the ribs plus most of the marinade into the pan and cook, turning frequently, for 30 minutes.

While the ribs are cooking, finely slice the spring onions on the diagonal. Place the ribs on a warmed serving plate then scatter the spring onions and strips of ginger over the top and serve with fresh salad leaves on the side.

Energy 309kcal/1297kJ; Protein 38.3g; Carbohydrate 8g, of which sugars 8g; Fat 14g, of which saturates 4.7g; Cholesterol 123mg; Calcium 46mg; Fibre 0.1g; Sodium 75mg

FISH AND SEAFOOD

GINGER, WHEN COMBINED WITH OTHER

DELICIOUS INGREDIENTS SUCH AS GARLIC,

LEMON JUICE, CHILLI AND FRESH HERBS, LENDS

ITS WONDERFUL FLAVOUR TO SUCCULENT

FISH BAKES AND STIR-FRIES

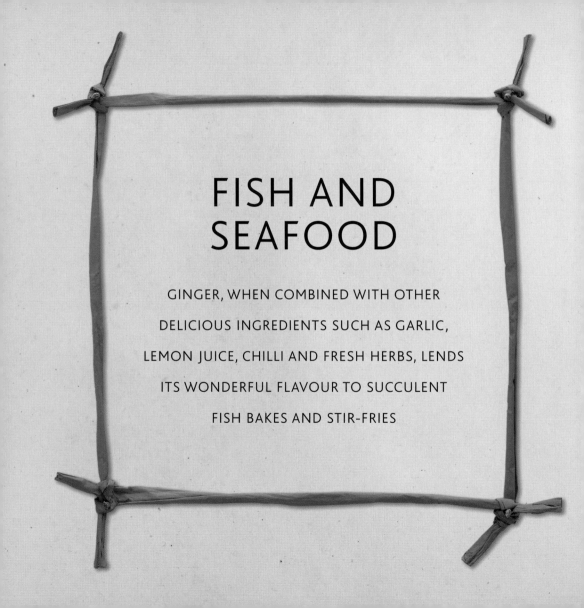

SALMON, SESAME AND GINGER FISHCAKES

These light fishcakes make a tempting appetizer served simply with a wedge of lime for squeezing over, but are also perfect for a light lunch or supper, served with a crunchy, refreshing salad.

Makes 25

500g/1¼lb salmon fillet, skinned and boned
45ml/3 tbsp dried breadcrumbs
30ml/2 tbsp mayonnaise
30ml/2 tbsp sesame seeds
30ml/2 tbsp light soy sauce
finely grated rind (zest) of 2 limes
10ml/2 tsp finely grated fresh root ginger
4 spring onions (scallions), finely sliced
vegetable oil, for frying
spring onion slivers, to garnish
lime wedges, to serve

Finely chop the salmon and place in a bowl. Add the breadcrumbs, mayonnaise, sesame seeds, soy sauce, lime zest, ginger and spring onions and use your fingers to mix well.

With wet hands, divide the mixture into 25 portions and shape each one into a small round cake. Place the cakes on a baking sheet, lined with baking parchment, cover and chill for several hours or overnight.

When you are ready to cook the fishcakes heat about 5cm/2in vegetable oil in a wok. Working in batches, shallow fry the fishcakes over a medium heat for 2–3 minutes on each side.

Drain the fishcakes well on kitchen paper and serve warm or at room temperature, garnished with spring onion slivers and plenty of lime wedges for squeezing over.

Energy 83kcal/343kJ; Protein 4.6g;
Carbohydrate 1.6g, of which sugars 0.2g;
Fat 6.5g, of which saturates 0.9g;
Cholesterol 11mg; Calcium 16mg;
Fibre 0.2g; Sodium 117mg.

STEAMED SCALLOPS WITH GINGER

This recipe uses two woks so that all the scallops can be cooked at the same time. For the best results, use the freshest scallops you can buy from your fishmonger.

Serves 4

24 king scallops in their shells,
    cleaned
15ml/1 tbsp very finely
    shredded fresh root ginger
5ml/1 tsp very finely chopped
    garlic
1 large red chilli, seeded and
    very finely chopped
15ml/1 tbsp light soy sauce
15ml/1 tbsp Chinese rice wine
a few drops of sesame oil
2–3 spring onions (scallions),
    very finely shredded
15ml/1 tbsp very finely chopped
    fresh chives
noodles or rice, to serve

Remove the scallops from their shells, then remove the membrane and hard white muscle from each one. Arrange the scallops on two plates. Rinse the shells, dry and set aside.

Fill two woks with 5cm/2in water and place a trivet in the base of each one. Bring to the boil.

Meanwhile, mix together the ginger, garlic, chilli, soy sauce, rice wine, sesame oil, spring onions and chives and spoon over the scallops.

Lower a plate of scallops into each of the woks. Turn the heat to low, cover and steam for 10–12 minutes, or until just cooked through.

Divide the scallops among four, or eight, of the reserved shells and serve immediately with noodles or rice.

Energy 157kcal/664kJ; Protein 29g; Carbohydrate 5g, of which sugars 1g; Fat 3g, of which saturates 1g; Cholesterol 56mg; Calcium 41mg; Fibre 0g; Sodium 432mg.

COOK'S TIP
If you would prefer not to shuck the scallops ask your local fishmonger to do this task.

SEARED TUNA WITH GINGER AND CHILLI

Tuna steaks are wonderful seared and presented slightly rare with a punchy sauce or salad. In this recipe the salad is served just warm as a bed for the tender tuna.

Serves 4
30ml/2 tbsp olive oil
5ml/1 tsp harissa
5ml/1 tsp clear honey
2.5ml/½ tsp salt
4 x 200g/7oz tuna steaks
lemon wedges, to serve

For the salad
30ml/2 tbsp olive oil
a little butter
25g/1oz fresh root ginger,
*   peeled and finely sliced*
2 garlic cloves, finely sliced
2 green chillies, seeded and
*   finely sliced*
6 spring onions (scallions), cut
*   into bitesize pieces*
2 large handfuls of watercress
juice of ½ lemon
salt and ground black pepper

Energy 428kcal/1788kJ; Protein 48g;
Carbohydrate 2g, of which sugars 2g;
Fat 25g, of which saturates 5g;
Cholesterol 56mg; Calcium 58mg; Fibre 0g;
Sodium 101mg.

Mix the olive oil, harissa, honey and salt, and rub it over the tuna steaks. Heat a frying pan, grease it with a little oil and sear the tuna steaks for about 2 minutes on each side. They should still be pink on the inside.

Keep the tuna warm while you quickly prepare the salad: heat the olive oil and butter in a heavy pan. Add the ginger, garlic, chillies and spring onions. Cook until the mixture begins to colour, then add the watercress. When the watercress begins to wilt, toss in the lemon juice and season well with salt and plenty of ground black pepper.

Tip the warm salad on to a serving dish or individual plates. Slice the tuna steaks and arrange on top of the salad. Serve immediately with lemon wedges for squeezing over.

Seared shellfish Prawns (shrimp) and scallops can be cooked in the same way. The shellfish will just need to be cooked through briefly – if cooked for too long they will become rubbery.

HALIBUT WITH LEEK AND GINGER

Generally fish should to be absolutely fresh, but halibut needs to mature for a day or two to bring out the flavour. The leek and ginger mixture is the perfect accompaniment to this fine fish steak.

Serves 4

2 leeks
50g/2oz piece fresh root ginger
4 halibut steaks, approximately
*   175g/6oz each (see Cook's*
*   Tip)*
15ml/1 tbsp olive oil
75g/3oz/6 tbsp butter
salt and ground black pepper
mashed potato, to serve

Trim the leeks, discarding the coarse outer leaves, the very dark green tops and the root end. Cut them into 5cm/2in lengths then slice into thin matchsticks. Wash thoroughly.

Peel the fresh ginger then slice it very thinly and cut the slices into thin sticks.

Dry the halibut steaks on kitchen paper. Heat a large pan with the olive oil and add 50g/2oz/4 tbsp of the butter. As it begins to bubble place the fish steaks carefully in the pan, skin side down. Allow the halibut to colour – this will take 3–4 minutes. Then turn the steaks over, reduce the heat and cook for about a further 10 minutes.

Remove the fish from the pan, set aside and keep warm. Add the leek and ginger to the pan, stir to mix then allow the leek to soften (they may colour slightly but this is fine). Once softened, season with a little salt and ground black pepper. Cut the remaining butter into small pieces then, off the heat, gradually stir into the pan.

To serve, place the halibut steaks on warmed plates and strew the leek and ginger mixture over the fish. Accompany with mashed potato.

Energy 364kcal/1520kJ; Protein 39.1g; Carbohydrate 2.7g, of which sugars 2.1g; Fat 21.9g, of which saturates 10.8g; Cholesterol 101mg; Calcium 75mg; Fibre 1.9g; Sodium 221mg.

COOK'S TIPS

• Ask your fishmonger for flattish halibut steaks and not too thick as you want to cook them in a pan on the stove and not in the oven. Also ask him or her to skin them for you.
• It doesn't matter if you leave a bit of skin on the ginger if it is very knobbly.

MEAT, POULTRY AND GAME

WHETHER STIR-FRIED WITH PORK, ROASTED

WITH DUCK OR MARINADED WITH BEEF

IN A CLASSIC CHINESE SAUCE, GINGER ADDS

WONDERFUL PUNGENCY TO ALL KINDS

OF MEAT AND POULTRY RECIPES

STIR-FRIED PORK WITH GINGER

Pork marries well with ginger, garlic and spring onions – three ingredients that are regarded as the essential basis of Chinese seasoning. Be lavish with the ginger as it is the hallmark of this dish.

Serves 4

250g/9oz pork rib-eye steak
30ml/2 tbsp sesame oil
30ml/2 tbsp vegetable oil
15ml/1 tbsp sliced garlic
40g/1½ oz fresh young root
*   ginger, sliced into very fine*
*   strips*
2 spring onions (scallions)
30ml/2 tbsp oyster sauce
5–10ml/1–2 tsp ground
*   black pepper*
30ml/2 tbsp Chinese rice wine
30ml/2 tbsp water

Using a sharp knife, cut the pork into thin strips. Place these on a board and tenderize them slightly, using a meat mallet or the blunt edge of a cleaver. Rub the strips with sesame oil and set them aside for about 15 minutes.

Heat the vegetable oil in a wok. Add the sliced garlic and ginger and fry for 1 minute, until pale brown. Do not let the garlic burn.

Add the pork strips and spring onions. Stir-fry for 2 minutes, then add the oyster sauce and black pepper. Stir over the heat for 2 minutes until the seasonings have been thoroughly absorbed by the pork.

Pour in the wine and water. Continue to cook, stirring, for 2 minutes, until the liquid bubbles and the pork is fully cooked. Spoon into a heated bowl and serve.

Energy 179kcal/747kJ; Protein 25.3g;
Carbohydrate 2.8g, of which sugars 2.1g;
Fat 7.4g, of which saturates 1.9g;
Cholesterol 71mg; Calcium 21mg; Fibre
0.7g; Sodium 614mg.

BRAISED BEEF STRIPS WITH SOY AND GINGER

Fine strips of braised beef are enhanced by a rich, dark soy and garlic sauce, with a piquant kick of root ginger. This dish makes an excellent side serving to accompany a larger stew or noodle dish.

Serves 2–3

450g/1lb beef flank
25g/1oz piece fresh root ginger, peeled
100ml/3½fl oz/scant ½ cup dark soy sauce
75g/3oz light muscovado (brown) sugar
12 garlic cloves, peeled
6 jalapeño chillies

COOK'S TIP
If you're using any beef cut other than the flank, the meat should be cut into thin strips or torn by hand to ensure that it is tender when cooked.

Bring a large pan of water to the boil and add the beef. Cook for around 40 minutes until tender. Drain the meat and rinse it in warm water. Leave the beef to cool, then roughly slice it into long strips about 5cm/2in long.

Place the peeled root ginger in a large pan with the beef and add 300ml/½ pint/1¼ cups water. Bring to the boil, cover and then reduce the heat and simmer for 30 minutes. Skim the fat from the surface of the liquid as the meat cooks. The liquid should have reduced to half its initial volume. Add the soy sauce, muscovado sugar and garlic, and simmer for a further 20 minutes. Then add the jalapeño chillies, and cook for a further 5 minutes.

Discard the root ginger, and serve in bowls with generous quantities of the garlic and chillies.

Energy 408kcal/1713kJ; Protein 37.8g; Carbohydrate 34.3g, of which sugars 29.1g; Fat 14.2g, of which saturates 5.7g; Cholesterol 87mg; Calcium 33mg; Fibre 1.4g; Sodium 2472mg.

CAMBODIAN CHICKEN WITH YOUNG GINGER

Ginger plays a big role in Cambodian cooking, particularly in the stir-fried dishes. Whenever possible, the juicier and more pungent young ginger is used.

Serves 4

30ml/2 tbsp groundnut (peanut) oil
3 garlic cloves, finely sliced in strips
50g/2oz fresh young root ginger, finely sliced in strips
2 Thai chillies, seeded and finely sliced in strips
4 chicken breasts or 4 boned chicken legs, skinned and cut into bitesize chunks
30ml/2 tbsp tuk prahoc, or fish sauce
10ml/2 tsp sugar
small bunch coriander (cilantro) stalks removed, roughly chopped
ground black pepper
jasmine rice, to serve

Heat a wok or heavy pan and add the oil. Add the garlic, ginger and chillies, and stir-fry until fragrant and golden. Add the chicken and toss it around the wok for 1–2 minutes.

Stir in the *tuk prahoc* and sugar, and stir-fry for a further 4–5 minutes until cooked. Season with pepper and add some of the fresh coriander.

Transfer the chicken to a serving dish and garnish with the remaining coriander. Serve hot with jasmine rice.

Energy 222Kcal/935kJ; Protein 36.4g; Carbohydrate 3g, of which sugars 2.9g; Fat 7.3g, of which saturates 1.1g; Cholesterol 105mg; Calcium 32mg; Fibre 0.6g; Sodium 100mg

COOK'S TIP
Young ginger is available in Chinese and South-east Asian markets.

ROAST DUCK LEGS WITH QUINCE, GINGER AND HONEY

The scented quince resembles a large, hard pear and often features with lamb or poultry, as in this typically Moroccan recipe. The ginger spice counterbalances the sweet honey in this rich dish.

Serves 4

4 duck legs
30ml/2 tbsp olive oil
2 lemons
600ml/1 pint/2½ cups water
2 quinces, quartered, cored
*   and peeled*
a little butter
25g/1oz fresh root ginger,
*   peeled and grated*
10ml/2 tsp ground cinnamon
30ml/2 tbsp clear honey
salt and ground black pepper
small bunch of fresh coriander
*   (cilantro), chopped, to serve*

Preheat the oven to 230°C/450°F/Gas 8. Rub the duck legs with half the olive oil, season, and place on a rack in a roasting pan. Roast in the oven for about 30 minutes until the skin is crisp and golden.

Meanwhile, squeeze the juice from ½ lemon and place in a pan. Add the water and bring to the boil. Add the quince quarters and simmer for about 15 minutes until tender. Drain and refresh, then cut each quince quarter into slices. Heat the remaining olive oil and butter and fry the quince slices until brown. Remove from the pan and keep warm.

Take the duck out of the oven and pour 30ml/2 tbsp of the duck fat into the pan in which the fruit was cooked. Stir in the ginger and cook for 1 minute, then add the cinnamon, honey and the remaining lemon juice. Pour in 30–45ml/2–3 tbsp water and stir until it bubbles up to make a small amount of sauce; remove from the heat.

Arrange the duck legs and quince slices on a plate and spoon the sauce over them. Sprinkle with fresh coriander and serve immediately.

Energy 328kcal/1369kJ; Protein 26g;
Carbohydrate 10g, of which sugars 9g;
Fat 21g, of which saturates 6g; Cholesterol
123mg; Calcium 42mg; Fibre 2.6g;
Sodium 220mg.

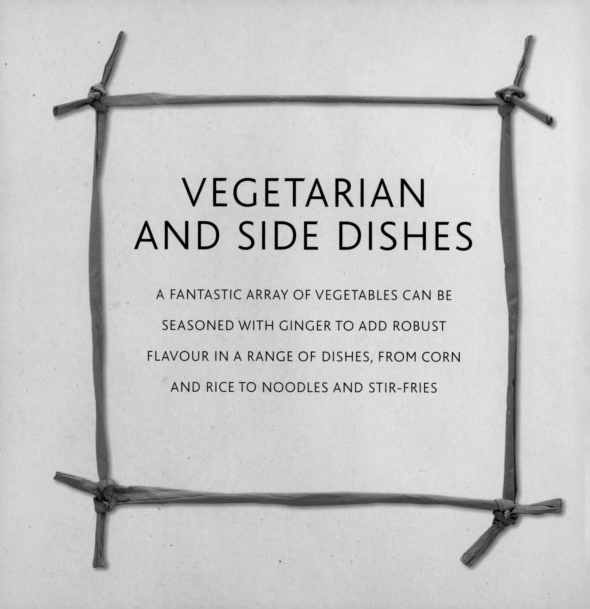

VEGETARIAN AND SIDE DISHES

A FANTASTIC ARRAY OF VEGETABLES CAN BE

SEASONED WITH GINGER TO ADD ROBUST

FLAVOUR IN A RANGE OF DISHES, FROM CORN

AND RICE TO NOODLES AND STIR-FRIES

ROYAL CORN CURRY

Corn is an extremely popular vegetable in northern India, where it is often mixed with chillies and ginger to make a warming vegetable side dish.

Serves 4

15ml/1 tbsp white poppy seeds
5ml/1 tsp coriander seeds
460ml/ tbsp sunflower oil or
  plain olive oil
4 green cardamom pods,
  bruised
1 large onion, finely chopped
10ml/2 tsp ginger purée
2 green chillies, finely chopped
  (seeded if you like)
2.5ml⅟₂ tsp ground turmeric
450g/1lb/2½ cups frozen corn,
  thawed and drained, or
  canned corn, drained and
  well rinsed
225ml/8fl oz/scant 1 cup full-
  fat (whole) milk
5ml/1 tsp salt, or to taste
110g/4oz fresh tomatoes,
  skinned and chopped
2.5ml⅟₂ tsp garam masala

Energy 368kcal/1539kJ; Protein 7.7g;
Carbohydrate 43.6g, of which sugars 21.6g;
Fat 19.4g, of which saturates 5.2g;
Cholesterol 8mg; Calcium 128mg; Fibre
4.4g; Sodium 343mg.

Grind the poppy seeds and coriander seeds in a coffee grinder until fine and set aside.

Heat the oil in a frying pan over a low heat and fry the cardamom pods gently for 25–30 seconds until they puff up, then increase the heat to medium and add the onion, ginger and chillies. Fry for 8–9 minutes, until the onion is lightly browned, stirring frequently to encourage even browning.

Add the turmeric and the ground seeds. Cook for a further minute and then add the corn, milk and salt. Let the mixture simmer gently for 8–10 minutes, stirring occasionally.

Add the tomatoes and garam masala and transfer the mixture to a serving dish.

SWEET AND HOT VEGETABLE NOODLES

This noodle dish has the colour of fire, but only the mildest suggestion of heat. Ginger and plum sauce give it a fruity flavour, while lime adds a delicious tang.

Serves 4

130g/4½oz dried rice noodles
30ml/2 tbsp groundnut (peanut) oil
2.5cm/1in piece fresh root ginger, sliced into thin batons
1 garlic clove, crushed
130g/4½oz drained canned bamboo shoots, sliced into thin batons
2 medium carrots, sliced into batons
130g/4½oz/1½ cups beansprouts
1 small white cabbage, shredded
30ml/2 tbsp Thai fish sauce
30ml/2 tbsp soy sauce
30ml/2 tbsp plum sauce
10ml/2 tsp sesame oil
15ml/1 tbsp palm sugar
juice of ½ lime
90g/3½oz mooli (daikon), sliced into thin batons
small bunch fresh coriander (cilantro), chopped
60ml/4 tbsp sesame seeds, toasted

Cook the noodles in a large pan of boiling water, following the instructions on the packet. Meanwhile, heat the oil in a wok or large frying pan and stir-fry the ginger and garlic for 2–3 minutes over a medium heat, until golden.

Drain the noodles and set them aside. Add the bamboo shoots to the wok, increase the heat and stir-fry for 5 minutes. Add the carrots, beansprouts and cabbage and cook for a further 5 minutes, until they are beginning to char on the edges.

Stir in the sauces, sesame oil, sugar and lime juice. Add the mooli and fresh coriander, toss to mix, then spoon into a warmed bowl, sprinkle with toasted sesame seeds and serve immediately.

Energy 368kcal/1530kJ; Protein 8.8g; Carbohydrate 45.8g, of which sugars 17.6g; Fat 16.5g, of which saturates 2.3g; Cholesterol 0mg; Calcium 200mg; Fibre 6.2g; Sodium 650mg.

STIR-FRIED PINEAPPLE WITH GINGER

This dish makes an interesting accompaniment to grilled meat or strongly-flavoured fish such as tuna or swordfish. It is similar to a fresh mango chutney, but with pineapple as the main ingredient.

Serves 4
1 pineapple
15ml/1 tbsp vegetable oil
2 garlic cloves, finely chopped
2 shallots, finely chopped
5cm/2in piece fresh root ginger,
    peeled and finely shredded
30ml/2 tbsp light soy sauce
juice of ½ lime
1 large fresh red chilli, seeded
    and finely shredded

VARIATION
This also tastes excellent
if peaches or nectarines
are substituted for the
diced pineapple. Use
three or four, depending
on their size.

Energy 110kcal/467kJ; Protein 1g;
Carbohydrate 20.8g, of which sugars 20.8g;
Fat 3.2g, of which saturates 0.3g;
Cholesterol 0mg; Calcium 37mg;
Fibre 2.4g; Sodium 538mg.

Trim and peel the pineapple. Cut out the core and dice the flesh.

Heat the oil in a wok or frying pan. Stir-fry the garlic and shallots over a medium heat for 2–3 minutes, until golden. Do not let the garlic burn or the dish will taste bitter.

Add the pineapple. Stir-fry for about 2 minutes, or until the pineapple cubes start to turn golden on the edges.

Add the shredded ginger, soy sauce, lime juice and chopped chilli. Toss together until well mixed. Cook over a low heat for a further 2 minutes, then serve.

STIR-FRIED CARROTS WITH MANGO AND GINGER

Ripe, sweet mango is divine with carrots and ginger in this spicy vegetable dish. The carrots are an excellent side dish for grilled meat or couscous but can be served on their own with yogurt.

Serves 4–6
15–30ml/1–2 tbsp olive oil
1 onion, chopped
25g/1oz fresh root ginger,
    peeled and chopped
2–3 garlic cloves, chopped
5–6 carrots, sliced
30–45ml/2–3 tbsp shelled
    pistachio nuts, roasted
5ml/1 tsp ground cinnamon
5–10ml/1–2 tsp ras el hanout
1 small firm, ripe mango, peeled
    and coarsely diced
small bunch of fresh coriander
    (cilantro), finely chopped
juice of ½ lemon, plus wedges
    to serve
salt

Heat the olive oil in a heavy frying pan or wok. Stir in the onion, ginger and garlic and fry for 1 minute. Add the carrots, tossing them in the pan to make sure that they are thoroughly mixed with the flavouring ingredients, and cook until they begin to brown.

Add the pistachio nuts, cinnamon and ras el hanout, then gently mix in the mango. Sprinkle with coriander, season with salt and pour over the lemon juice. Serve immediately with a lemon wedge.

Energy 89kcal/371kJ; Protein 1.7g; Carbohydrate 8.2g, of which sugars 7.5g; Fat 5.7g, of which saturates 0.8g; Cholesterol 0mg; Calcium 23mg; Fibre 2.2g; Sodium 47mg.

STIR-FRIED ASPARAGUS WITH GALANGAL

One of the culinary legacies of French colonization in Vietnam and Cambodia is asparagus. Today it is grown in Vietnam and finds its way into stir-fries in both countries.

Serves 2–4

30ml/2 tbsp groundnut
 (peanut) oil
2 garlic cloves, finely chopped
2 Thai chillies, seeded and finely
 chopped
25g/1oz galangal, finely
 shredded
1 lemon grass stalk, trimmed
 and finely sliced
350g/12oz fresh asparagus
 stalks, trimmed
30ml/2 tbsp tuk trey (fish sauce)
30ml/2 tbsp soy sauce
5ml/1 tsp sugar
30ml/2 tbsp unsalted roasted
 peanuts, finely chopped
small bunch fresh coriander
 (cilantro), finely chopped

VARIATION

This recipe also works well
with broccoli, green beans
and courgettes (zucchini),
cut into strips.

Heat a wok and add the oil. Stir in the garlic, chillies, galangal and lemon grass and stir-fry until they begin to turn golden.

Add the asparagus and stir-fry for a further 1–2 minutes, until it is just tender but not too soft.

Stir in the *tuk trey*, soy sauce and sugar. Stir in the peanuts and fresh coriander and serve immediately.

Energy 117Kcal/482kJ; Protein 5g; Carbohydrate 3.3g, of which sugars 2.7g; Fat 9g, of which
saturates 1g; Cholesterol 0mg; Calcium 30mg; Fibre 2g; Sodium 535mg

GARLIC AND GINGER RICE WITH CORIANDER

Although many Asian dishes serve plain rice as an accompaniment, it is particularly tasty when fragrant with the flavours of ginger and herbs.

Serves 4–6

15ml/1 tbsp vegetable or groundnut (peanut) oil

2–3 garlic cloves, finely chopped

25g/1oz fresh root ginger, finely chopped

225g/8oz/generous 1 cup long grain rice, rinsed in several bowls of water and drained

900ml/1½ pints/3¾ cups chicken stock

small bunch fresh coriander (cilantro), finely chopped

Heat the oil in a clay pot or heavy pan. Stir in the garlic and ginger and fry until golden. Stir in the rice and allow it to absorb the flavours for 1–2 minutes. Pour in the stock and stir to make sure the rice doesn't stick. Bring the stock to the boil, then reduce the heat.

Scatter the coriander over the surface of the stock, cover the pan, and leave to cook gently for 20–25 minutes, until the rice has absorbed all the liquid. Turn off the heat and gently fluff up the rice to mix in the coriander. Cover and leave to infuse for 10 minutes before serving.

Energy 151Kcal/632kJ; Protein 3g; Carbohydrate 30g, of which sugars 0g; Fat 2g, of which saturates 0.3g; Cholesterol 0mg; Calcium 9mg; Fibre 0.1g; Sodium 124mg

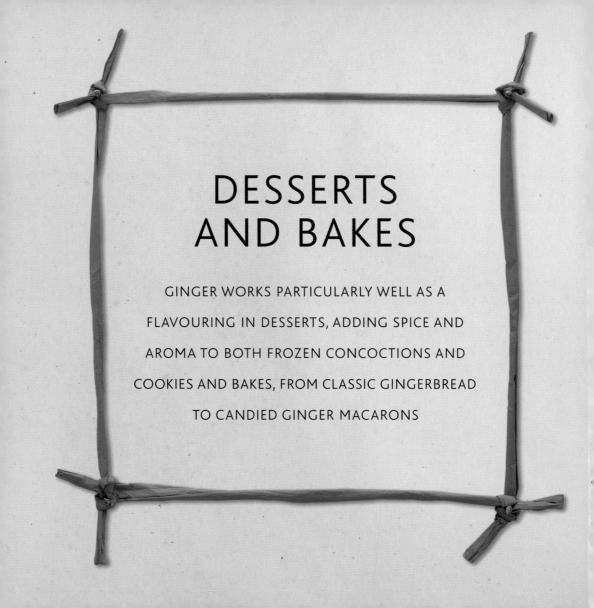

DESSERTS AND BAKES

GINGER WORKS PARTICULARLY WELL AS A
FLAVOURING IN DESSERTS, ADDING SPICE AND
AROMA TO BOTH FROZEN CONCOCTIONS AND
COOKIES AND BAKES, FROM CLASSIC GINGERBREAD
TO CANDIED GINGER MACARONS

GINGER AND KIWI SORBET

Freshly grated root ginger gives a lively, aromatic flavour to sorbets and ice creams. Here, it is combined with kiwi fruit to make a refreshing sorbet.

Serves 6

150g/2oz fresh root ginger
115g/4oz/½ cup caster
*   (superfine) sugar*
300ml/½ pint/1¼ cups water
5 kiwi fruit
fresh mint sprigs or chopped
*   kiwi fruit, to decorate*

COOK'S TIP
For best results, ensure that your original mixture is chilled until it is very cold before freezing or churning in an ice cream maker.

Energy 100kcal/426kJ; Protein 0.7g;
Carbohydrate 25.3g, of which sugars 25.2g;
Fat 0.3g, of which saturates 0g;
Cholesterol 0mg; Calcium 23mg; Fibre 1g;
Sodium 3mg.

Peel the ginger and grate it finely. Put the sugar and water in a saucepan and heat gently until the sugar has dissolved. Add the ginger and cook for 1 minute, then leave to cool. Strain into a bowl and chill.

Peel the kiwi fruit and blend until smooth. Add the puree to the chilled syrup and mix well.

By hand: Pour the mixture into a container and freeze for 3–4 hours, beating twice as it thickens. Return to the freezer until ready to serve.

Using an ice cream maker: Churn the mixture until it thickens. Transfer to a plastic tub or similar freezerproof container and freeze until ready to serve.

Spoon into glasses, decorate with mint sprigs or chopped kiwi fruit, and serve.

GINGERED SEMI-FREDDO

This Italian ice cream is made with a boiled sugar syrup rather than a traditional egg custard and is generously speckled with chopped stem ginger. It will stay soft when frozen.

Serves 6

4 egg yolks
115g/4oz/generous ½ cup caster (superfine) sugar
5ml/1 tsp cornflour (cornstarch)
120ml/4 fl oz/½ cup cold water
300ml/½ pints/1½ cups double (heavy) cream
115g/4oz/⅔ cup drained stem ginger, finely chopped, plus extra slices, to decorate
45ml/3 tbsp whisky (optional)

COOK'S TIP

Semi-freddo looks wonderful in chocolate cases, made by spreading melted chocolate over squares of non-stick baking parchment and then draping them over upturned tumbers. Peel the paper off when the chocolate has set and turn the cases the right way up.

Put the egg yolks in a large heatproof bowl and whisk until frothy. Bring a pan of water to the boil and simmer gently.

Mix the sugar, cornflour and measured cold water in a pan and heat gently, stirring occasionally, until the sugar has dissolved.

Increase the heat and boil for 4–5 minutes without stirring until the syrup registers 115°C/239°F on a sugar thermometer. Alternatively, test by dropping a little of the syrup into a cup of cold water. Pour the water away. You should be able to mould the syrup into a ball.

Put the bowl of egg yolks over the pan of simmering water and stir in the sugar syrup. Continue whisking until the mixture is very thick. Remove from the heat and whisk until cool.

Whip the cream and lightly fold it into the yolk mixture, with the chopped ginger and whisky, if using.

By hand: Pour into a plastic tub or similar freezerproof container and freeze for 1 hour.

Using an ice cream maker: Churn the mixture until it thickens.

Stir the semi-freddo to bring any ginger that has sunk to the bottom of the tub to the top, then return to the freezer for 5–6 hours until firm. Scoop into dishes or chocolate cases (see Cook's Tip). Decorate with slices of ginger.

Energy 371kcal/1539kJ; Protein 3g; Carbohydrate 22.4g, of which sugars 22.3g; Fat 30.6g, of which saturates 17.8g; Cholesterol 203mg; Calcium 55mg; Fibre 0.5g; Sodium 23mg.

GINGER WINE AND RHUBARB TORTE

Rhubarb is not often used in iced desserts, but this torte uses it in a classic partnership with ginger. The result is a refreshingly tart flavour, making it perfect for those who prefer less sweet desserts.

Serves 8

500g/1¼ lb rhubarb, trimmed
115g/4oz/½ cup caster
  (superfine) sugar
30ml/1 tbsp water
200g/7oz/scant 1 cup cream
  cheese
300ml/½ pints/1½ cups double
  (heavy) cream
150g/5 oz/¼ cup stem ginger,
  finely chopped
a few drops of pink food
  colouring (optional)
250ml/8fl oz/1 cup ginger wine
175g/6oz sponge (lady) fingers
fresh mint or lemon balm
  sprigs, dusted with icing
  (confectioners') sugar,
  to decorate

Chop the rhubarb roughly and put it in a pan with the sugar and water. Cover and cook very gently for 5–8 minutes until the rhubarb is just tender. Process or blend untiil smooth, then leave to cool.

Beat the cream cheese in a bowl until softened. Stir in the cream, rhubarb purée and ginger, then a little food colouring, if you like. Line a 900g/1lb/6-8 cup loaf tin (pan) with clear film (plastic wrap).

By hand: Pour the mixture into a shallow container and freeze for approximately 1 hour, until firm.

Using an ice cream maker: Churn in an ice cream maker until firm.

Pour the ginger wine into a shallow dish. Spoon a thin layer of ice cream over the bottom of the tin. Working quickly, dip the sponge fingers in the ginger wine, then lay them lengthways over the ice cream in a single layer. Trim the sponge fingers to fit.

Spread another layer of ice cream over the biscuits. Repeat the process, adding two to three more layers and finishing with ice cream. Cover and freeze overnight.

Transfer to the refrigerator 30 minutes before serving, to soften the torte slightly. Briefly dip in very hot water then invert it onto a flat dish. Peel off the clear film and decorate with sprigs of fresh mint or lemon balm, dusted with icing sugar.

COOK'S TIP
Taste the rhubarb mixture just before churning it and add a little sugar if you find the flavour too tart.

Energy 398kcal/1658kJ; Protein 3.9g; Carbohydrate 29.4g, of which sugars 25.2g; Fat 26.8g, of which saturates 16.2g; Cholesterol 100mg; Calcium 132mg; Fibre 1.2g; Sodium 111mg.

GINGERBREAD COOKIES

Golden gingerbread is often used to shape cookies as they can be thinly rolled and have a firm texture. Royal icing is traditionally used to pipe decorations onto gingerbread.

Makes 12 cookies
175g/6oz/1½ cups plain (all-purpose) flour
1.5ml/¼ tsp bicarbonate of soda (baking soda)
a pinch of salt
5ml/1 tsp ground ginger
5ml/1 tsp ground cinnamon
60ml/4 tbsp unsalted butter, cubed
75g/3oz/6 tbsp caster (superfine) sugar
30ml/2 tbsp maple or golden (light corn) syrup
1 egg yolk, beaten

For the royal icing
1 egg white
200–225g/7–8oz/1⅔–2 cups icing (confectioners') sugar

Energy 190kcal/806kJ; Protein 2g;
Carbohydrate 37g, of which sugars 26g;
Fat 4.9g, of which saturates 2.8g;
Cholesterol 30mg; Calcium 68mg; Fibre
0.6g; Sodium 99mg

Preheat the oven to 180°C/350°F/Gas 4. Sift together the flour, bicarbonate of soda, salt and spices. Rub the butter into the flour in a large bowl, until the mixture resembles fine breadcrumbs. Alternatively, blend in a food processor. Add the sugar, syrup and egg yolk and mix or process to a firm dough. Knead lightly. Wrap and chill for 30 minutes.

Roll out onto a lightly floured surface to about 5mm/¼ in depth and cut out the required shapes using pastry cutters. Bake on a lightly oiled baking tray for about 12 minutes, until they are just beginning to colour around the edges.

Royal icing: Beat the egg white. Beat in the sugar, a little at a time, until the mixture is smooth and forms soft peaks. Transfer to a bowl and cover the surface with clear film (plastic wrap), to prevent a crust from forming. Fill a paper piping bag with the icing, snip off the tip and drizzle the icing onto the cookies according to your chosen design. Royal icing will keep in the refrigerator for up to three days.

COURGETTE AND DOUBLE-GINGER TEA BREAD

Both fresh and preserved ginger are used to flavour this unusual tea bread. It is delicious served warm, cut into thick slices and spread with butter or margarine.

Serves 8–10

3 eggs
225g/8oz/generous 1 cup caster (superfine) sugar
250ml/8fl oz/1 cup sunflower oil
5ml/1 tsp vanilla extract
15ml/1 tbsp syrup from a jar of stem ginger
225g/8oz courgettes (zucchini), grated
2.5cm/1in piece fresh root ginger, grated
350g/12oz/3 cups plain (all-purpose) flour
5ml/1 tsp baking powder
pinch of salt
5ml/1 tsp ground cinnamon
2 pieces stem ginger, chopped
15ml/1 tbsp demerara (raw) sugar

Energy 502kcal/2107kJ; Protein 7.1g;
Carbohydrate 67.3g, of which sugars 34g;
Fat 24.6g, of which saturates 3.3g;
Cholesterol 71mg; Calcium 95mg; Fibre
1.6g; Sodium 35mg.

Preheat the oven to 190°C/325°F/Gas 5. Beat together the eggs and sugar until light and fluffy. Slowly beat in the oil until the mixture forms a batter. Mix in the vanilla extract and ginger syrup, then stir in the courgettes and fresh ginger.

Sift together the flour, baking powder and salt into a large bowl. Add the cinnamon and mix well, then stir the dried ingredients into the courgette mixture.

Lightly grease a 900g/2lb loaf tin (pan) and pour in the courgette mixture. Smooth and level the top, then sprinkle the chopped stem ginger and demerara sugar over the surface.

Bake for 1 hour until a skewer inserted into the centre comes out clean. Leave the cake in the tin to cool for about 20 minutes, then turn out on to a wire rack.

GINGERBREAD CAKE

This moreish cake is flavoured with Lebkuchen mix, which is a combination of 2.5ml/½ tsp ground cloves, cinnamon, ginger, cardamom, allspice, anise seed, star anise and nutmeg.

Makes 30 squares

300g/11oz/scant 3 cups hazelnuts
300g/11oz/1½ cups soft brown sugar
5 eggs
150g/5oz/10 tbsp butter, melted
100g/3½oz/½ cup honey
500g/1¼lb/5 cups plain (all-purpose) flour
25ml/5 tsp baking powder
25g/1oz Lebkuchen spice mix

Preheat the oven to 160°C/325°F/Gas 3 and line a 40x30cm/16x12in baking tray with baking parchment.

Heat a frying pan over medium heat and toast the hazelnuts, moving them around so that they brown evenly. Remove from the heat, cool, then chop finely.

Beat the sugar with the eggs until the mixture is light and thick. Stir in the melted butter, the honey and the chopped hazelnuts. Sift the flour with the baking powder and spice mix and fold into the mixture.

Pour the batter into the prepared tray. Bake in the preheated oven for about 45 minutes. Take it out and leave to cool in the tin before cutting into squares.

COOK'S TIP
If you like, melt some chocolate and spread it over the gingerbread once it has cooled.

Energy 741kcal/3106kJ; Protein 14.1g;
Carbohydrate 89.1g, of which sugars 45.4g;
Fat 38.9g, of which saturates 11.5g;
Cholesterol 144mg; Calcium 166mg; Fibre
3.8g; Sodium 171mg

CANDIED GINGER AND LIME MACARONS

Sweet with a hint of warming ginger spiciness, these macaron shells are perfect with a citrus filling.
The lime buttercream looks stunning when coloured a vivid green.

Makes 12 macarons
For the shells
60g/2¼oz egg whites (2 eggs)
60g/2¼oz/generous ¼ cup
  caster (superfine) sugar
7.5ml/1½ tsp egg white powder
120g/4¼oz/generous 1 cup
  icing (confectioners') sugar
60g/2¼oz/generous ½ cup
  ground almonds
1.5ml/¼ tsp ground ginger
orange food colouring gel
10g/¼oz crystallized stem
  ginger, cut into small cubes,
  to decorate

For the filling
80g/3¾oz/scant ¾ cup icing
  (confectioners') sugar
40g/1½oz/3 tbsp unsalted
  butter, softened
10ml/2 tsp lime juice
finely grated rind (zest) of ½
  lime
green food colouring gel

Line a baking tray with non-stick baking parchment. Fit a piping (pastry) bag with a plain round tip.

Place the egg whites in a clean bowl, and sift the caster sugar and egg white powder over the egg whites. Whisk with an electric mixer until stiff peaks form.

In a separate bowl, sift together the icing sugar, ground almonds and ginger. Add the egg white mixture to the almond mixture. Dip a cocktail stick (toothpick) into the colouring gel, and scrape this on to the tip of a spatula. Use the spatula to fold the mixture gently until it falls in ribbons when lifted with the spatula.

Fill the piping bag with the mixture and pipe 24 4cm/1½in rounds on to the lined baking tray. Top half of the shells with 3 pieces of crystallized stem ginger (these will be the tops). Preheat the oven to 130°C/250°F/Gas ½, and leave the baking tray out in a warm, dry room for at least 15 minutes.

Place the tray in the middle of the oven and bake for 10 minutes. Remove from the oven and allow to cool.

To make the lime buttercream filling, place the icing sugar and butter in a bowl, and whisk until crumbly. Add the lime juice, grated lime rind and a little green food colouring, and whisk until the filling is smooth.

To fill the macarons, place a teaspoonful of lime buttercream on to the flat side of an undecorated macaron shell and top with the flat side of a decorated macaron shell. Repeat to make 12 macarons.

Energy 4665kcal/19743kJ; Protein 15g; Carbohydrate 955g, of which sugars 955g; Fat 114g, of which saturates 75g; Cholesterol 330mg; Calcium 841mg; Fibre 0g; Sodium 1157mg

RHUBARB MUFFINS WITH GINGER

The shiny candied strips of scarlet rhubarb and paper-thin slices of stem ginger add a colourful topping to these muffins. Extra slices of stem ginger may be added to decorate the cooled muffins.

Makes 9–10 tall muffins

275g/10oz rhubarb, cleaned
30ml/2 tbsp syrup from a jar of preserved stem ginger
1 piece preserved stem ginger, chopped
50g/2oz/4 tbsp demerara (raw) sugar
150g/5oz/1¼ cups plain (all-purpose) flour
75g/3oz/¾ cup spelt flour
50g/2oz/¼ cup caster (superfine) sugar
10ml/2 tsp baking powder
2.5ml/½ tsp bicarbonate of soda (baking soda)
5ml/1 tsp ground ginger
120ml/4fl oz/½ cup low-fat natural (plain) yogurt
1 egg, lightly beaten

For the topping

15g/½oz/1 tbsp butter
15ml/1 tbsp ginger syrup
15ml/1 tbsp caster (superfine) sugar
1 piece stem ginger, finely sliced

Slice 175g/6oz rhubarb and put in a pan with 30ml/2 tbsp water, the ginger syrup, stem ginger and demerara sugar.

Bring to the boil, stirring. Lower the heat and simmer until soft, 2–3 minutes. Set aside.

Preheat the oven to 180°C/350°F/Gas 4. Line dariole moulds with tall paper cases (see Cook's Tip). Sift the dry ingredients together into a large bowl.

In another bowl, beat the yogurt and egg together. Stir in the cooked rhubarb and juices and mix into the dry ingredients. Divide the batter between the paper cases.

To make the topping, heat the butter, ginger syrup, 15ml/1 tbsp water and sugar in a small frying pan over a medium heat and stir until the sugar dissolves.

Cut the rest of the rhubarb into short fine strips and lightly stir them in the syrup. Leave to soften for 2 minutes, then add the stem ginger slices until warmed through. Remove from the heat. Add in small piles to the centre of the muffin tops and bake for 20 minutes until golden.

COOK'S TIP: Dariole moulds or tall, slim muffin tins are lined with pleated cake cases cut to size from paper liners used for loaf tins.

Energy 152kcal/646kJ; Protein 3.9g; Carbohydrate 31.1g, of which sugars 15g; Fat 2.3g, of which saturates 1.1g; Cholesterol 23mg; Calcium 82mg; Fibre 1.5g; Sodium 42mg.

GINGER GUMDROPS

Gumdrops are dense and chewy. They can be made in an assortment of colours and flavours. These are made with spicy candied ginger, which creates a gumdrop with a little bite.

Makes about 800g/1¾lb

water or oil, for greasing
20g/¾oz powdered gelatin
100ml/3½fl oz/scant ½ cup
cold water
400g/14oz/2 cups caster
(superfine) sugar
100ml/3½fl oz/scant ½ cup hot
water
15ml/1 tbsp lemon juice
100g/3¾oz candied ginger,
finely chopped
50g/2oz/½ cup cornflour
(cornstarch)
50g/2oz/½ cup icing
(confectioners') sugar

COOK'S TIP
Use a tiny cookie cutter to cut the gumdrops. Have a dish of hot water to hand to dip the cutter into occasionally. This will help prevent the cutter from sticking to the gumdrops.

Sprinkle a 20cm/8in square cake tin (pan) with water or lightly grease it with oil and line it with clear film. Set aside.

Put the gelatin in a small bowl and add the cold water. Stir to dissolve.

Put the sugar and hot water in a pan, stir to dissolve, then bring to the boil. Boil for 10 minutes.

Add the soaked gelatin and boil for a further 15 minutes.

Add the lemon juice and ginger, remove from the heat and leave to cool slightly. Pour into the tin. Leave to set for 24 hours.

Turn the mixture out on to a board. Cut into small rounds (see Cook's Tip). Transfer to a cooling rack and allow to dry for a couple of hours.

Dust all over with a mixture of the cornflour and icing sugar, then serve. Store in an airtight container.

Energy 2269kcal/9675kJ; Protein 19.8g; Carbohydrate 582.6g, of which sugars 536.6g; Fat 0.3g, of which saturates 0.1g; Cholesterol 0mg; Calcium 302mg; Fibre 1g; Sodium 80mg.

INDEX